Weather Words

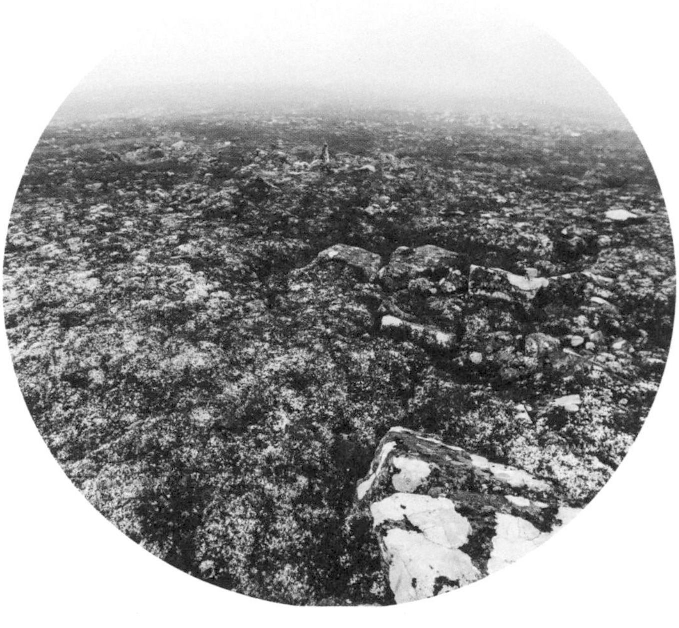

rain

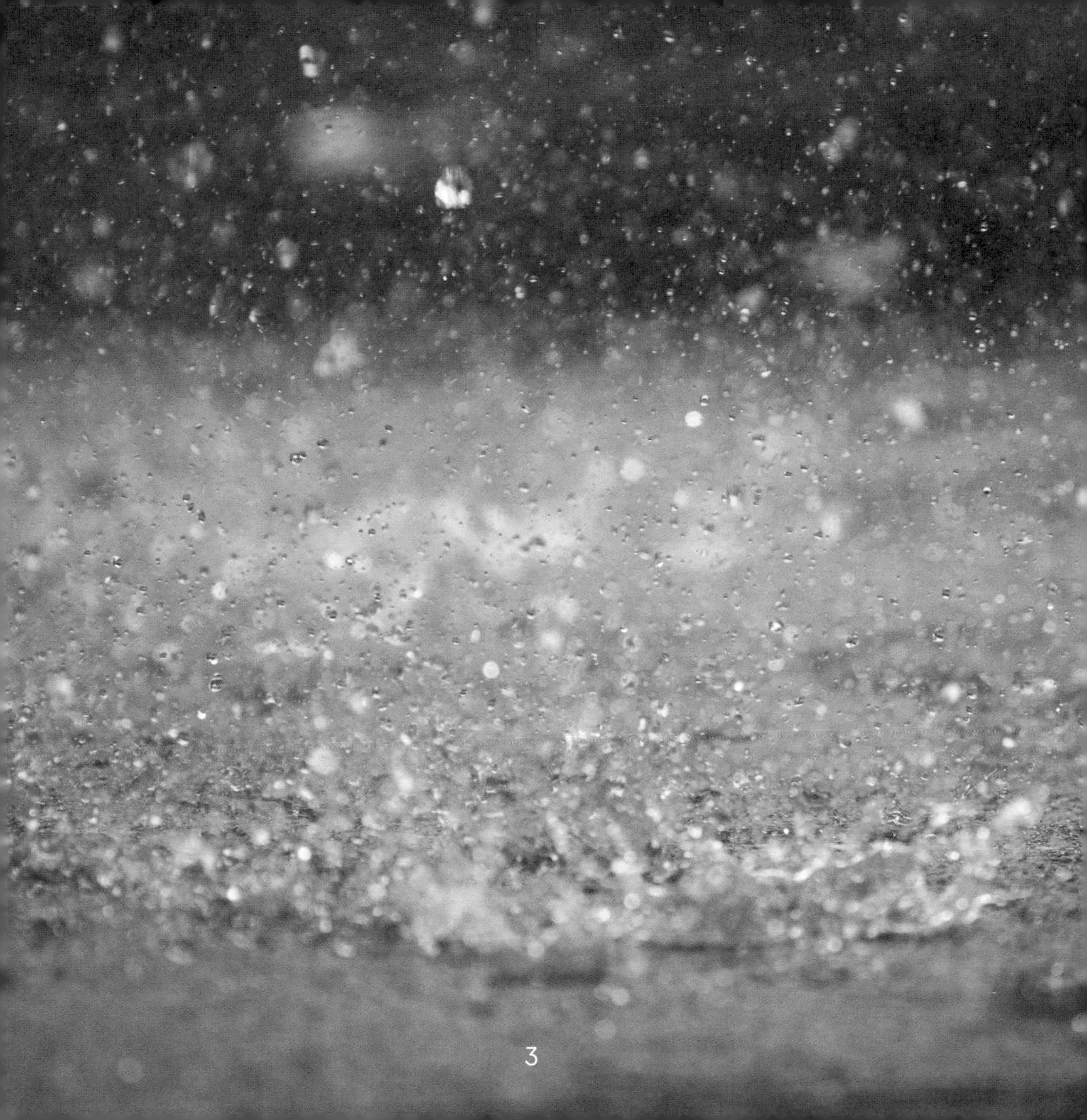

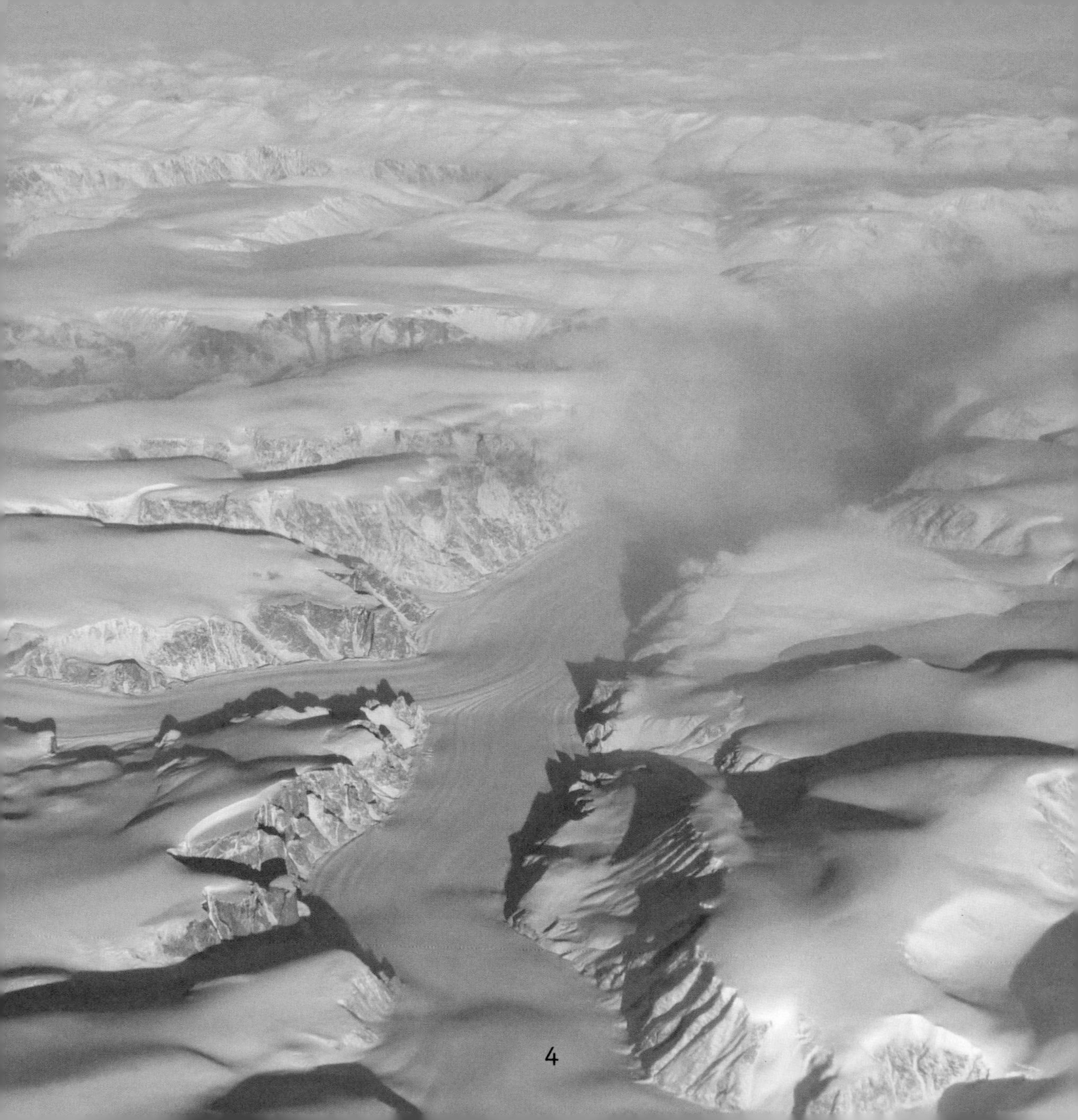

snow

lightning

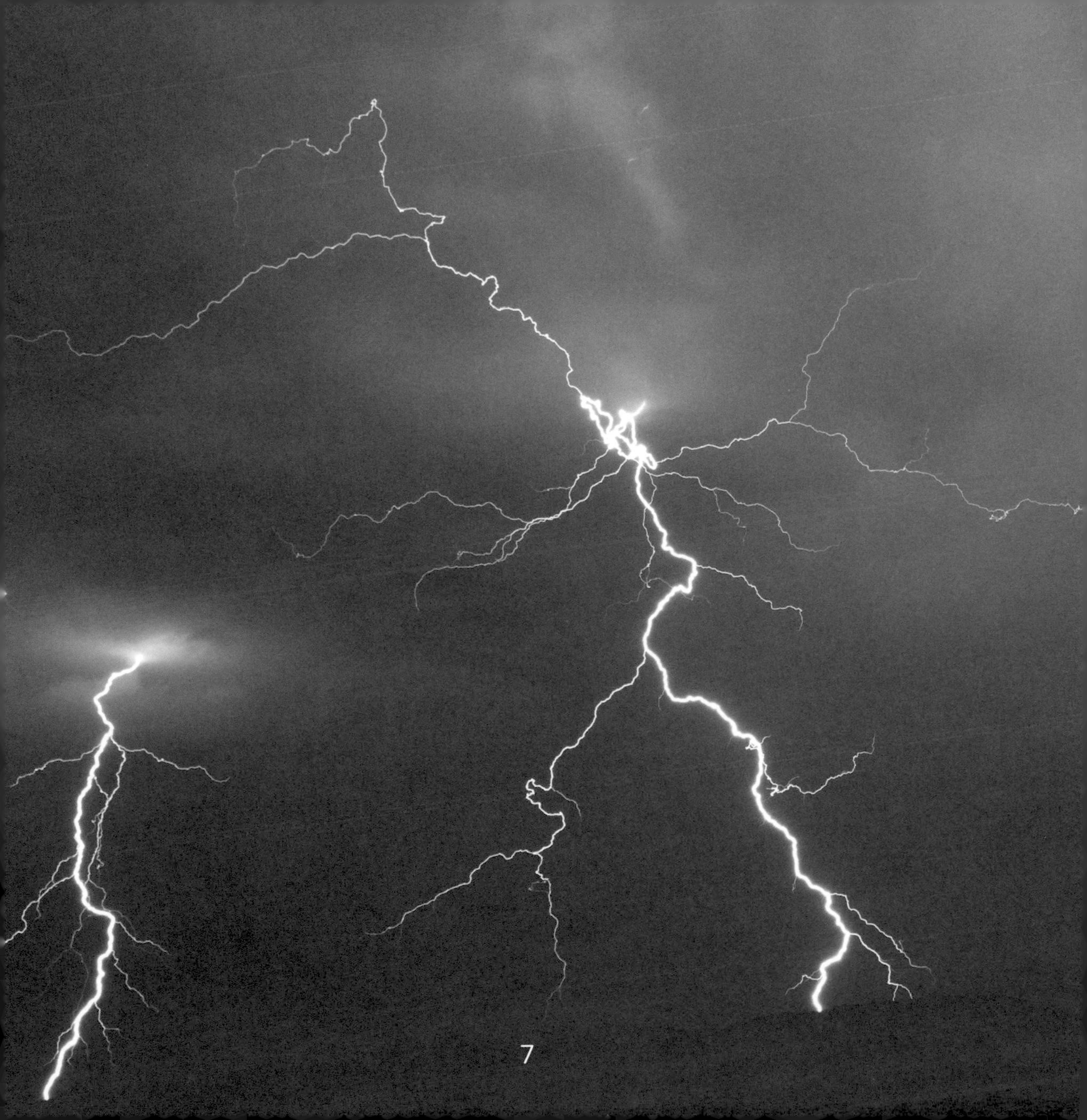

clouds

fog

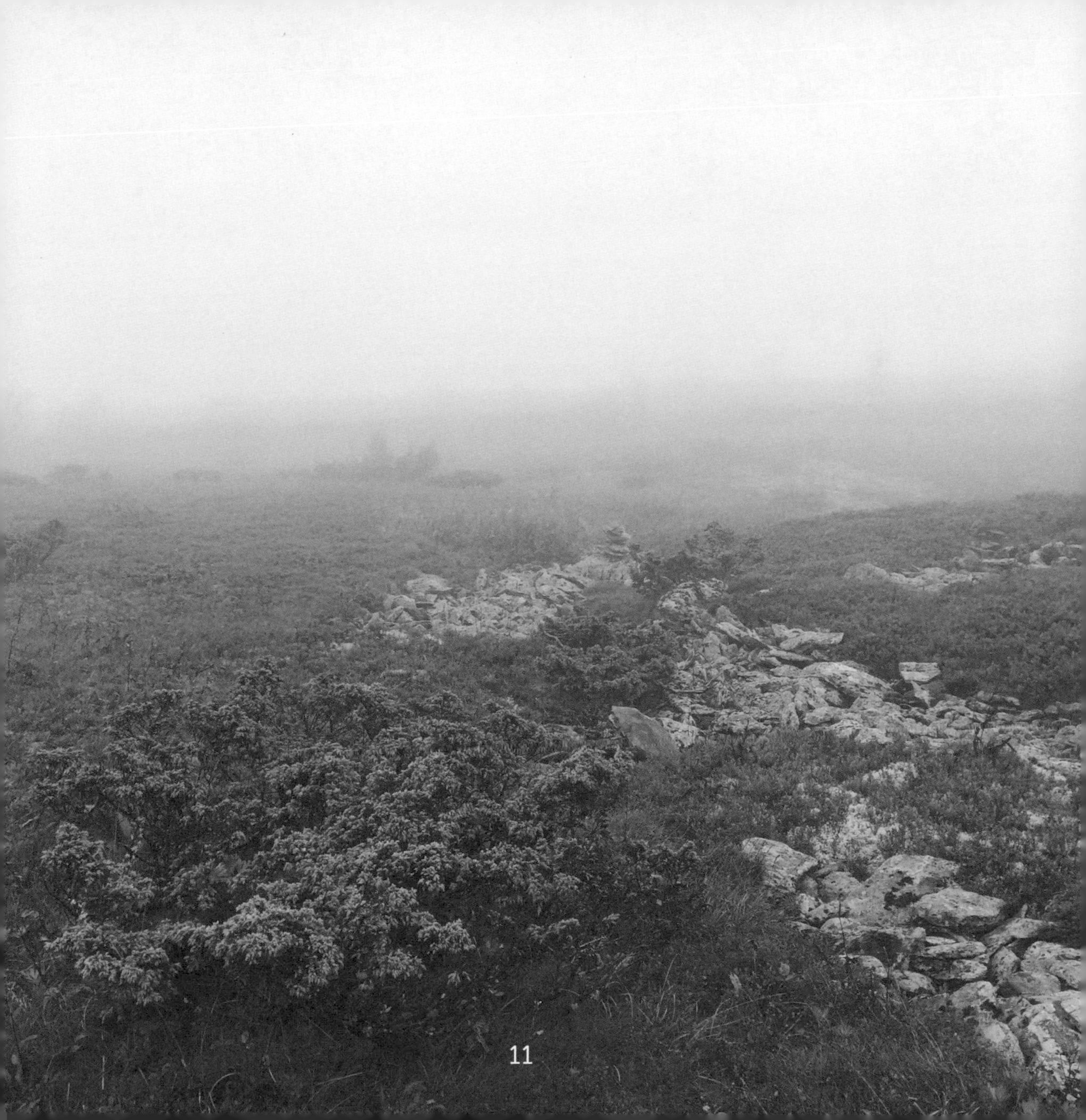

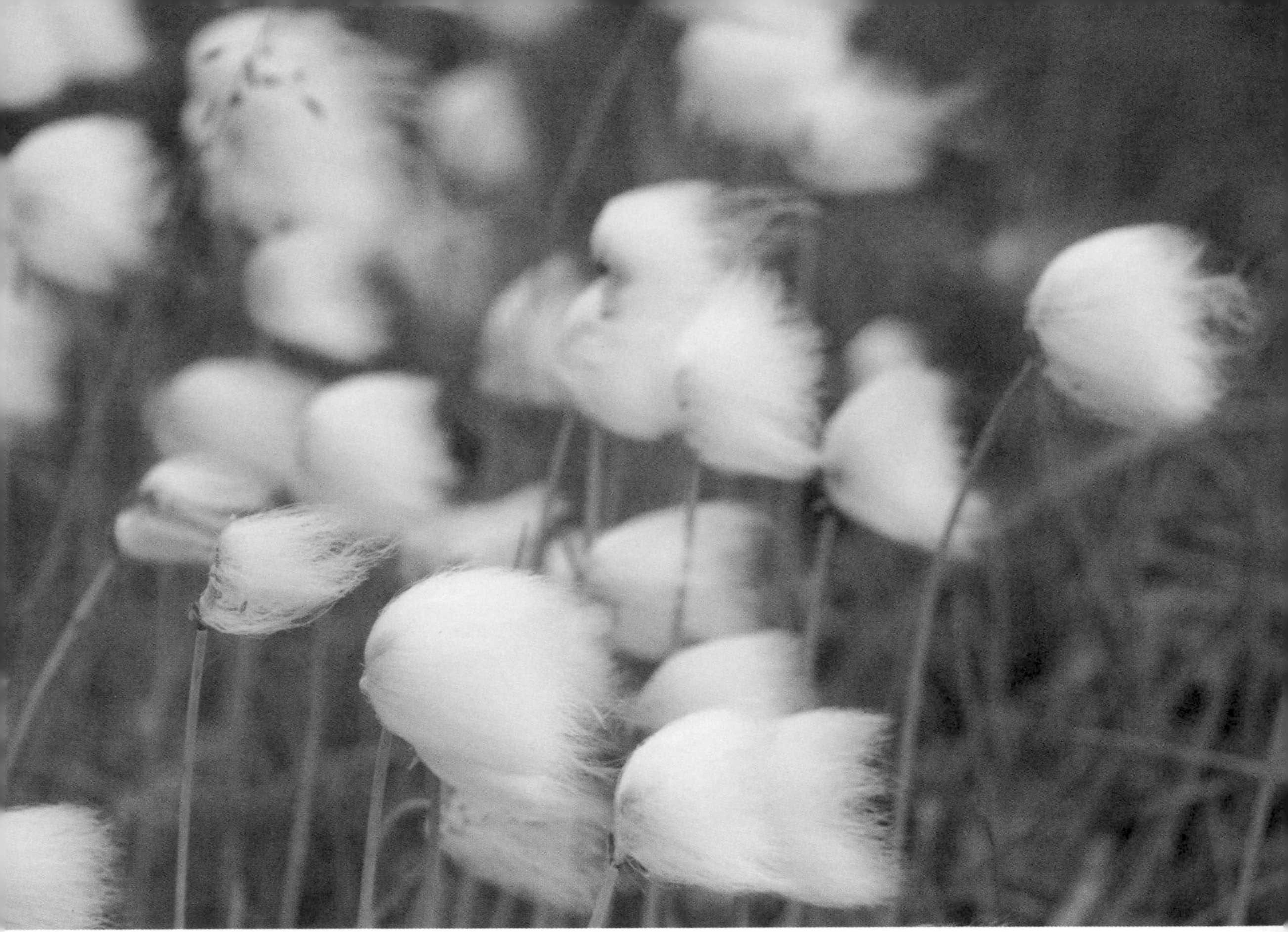

wind